GLOBAL INDIAN SCHOOL

Chairman   : Mr. Mohanachandran T
                    Mr. Babu T
Principal   : Mrs. Malathi Das
Vice Principal   : Mrs. Sobha Mohan
Vice Principal   : Mrs. Sindu Anand
  (Academics)

OBJECTIVE

The motto of the Global Indian School is to help students to develop to their potential.

EDUCATION BUILDS THE MAN WHO BUILDS THE NATION.
MISSION

To impart knowledge through modern methods

To assimilate knowledge through connected research. To groom future leaders sensitive to environment.

To encourage critical and innovative thinking.

VISION

Our vision coincides with the UAE education vision of Inclusive Education. Our vision is to make all the students in the school to be high achievers while helping the community and to have a proper value system. We want all our students to go to the University an earn tertiary qualifications. Year after year we are moving towards attaining our objective of all the students appearing for the board examinations obtaining Distinction (+75%) marks.

THE SCHOOL AND THE COMMUNITY

GLOBAL INDIAN SCHOOL AJMAN provides an environment of a family, where academics and value systems go hand in hand in an atmosphere of mutual trust and love. It is quite evident from the way the students, teachers and leaders of the school interact with each other.

Teachers continuously try to arouse the curiosity in the child and helps to bring out the inborn talent in them. Commencing in 1988 as Indian School Ajman, the school has earned a name all over the gulf as a school of high academic caliber. Students from the school occupy coveted positions in companies like McKinsey Consulting, Deloitte, E&Y, Apollo Hospital etc. Our principal took the initiative to bring together all the CBSE schools in the Gulf under the umbrella of Council of CBSE Schools in the Gulf which provides valuable collaboration among school

Adress: Al Hamidiya Road Jurf 2
Telephone :06 7444150
E Email : info@gisajman.com

English Language
A Kaleidoscope of Poetic Wihspers
(Collection of Poems)
Compiled by
Global Indian School Ajman

Published in November 2023
by Decan Imprint Publishing Co.
Reg. Off: Sharjah Publishing City
Free Zone Sharjah, UAE.
Phone: 00971-551830334
Email : decanimprint@gmail.com

Cover Design : Aromal O P

Printed at
Manipal Technologies Ltd.

13/23-24/Sl.No.13/50/NS 18.6
ISBN 978-93-5973-320-3

A KALEIDOSCOPE OF POETIC WHISPERS

WHISPERS

(Collection of Poems)

Compiled by

Global Indian School Ajman

DECANIMPRINT

Congratulations to the young talents making their mark in the world of literature. I am very proud to see my students utilizing this opportunity by submitting their inspiring short stories and poetry.

Global Indian School has always encouraged students to explore their creative capabilities and I'm looking forward to watching them flourish.

All the best!

Mrs. Malathi Das
Principal

It gives me immense joy to see the young minds of Global Indian School nurturing their talent and channelling their inner inspiration.

I always tell our students that from the moment you put pen to paper, you're a poet! And like other poets, your goal is to express yourself.

Each poetry in this book offers content around a different, compelling theme, filled with thoughtful questions, inspiration for composition, and interactive prompts to learn about themselves and the world around them.

I wish to congratulate our students and the editorial team for their team effort and thank your team for giving us the opportunity to be part of this mega project.

Best wishes,

Mrs. Sindu Anand
Vice Principal (Academics)

EDITORIAL TEAM

Unveiling the Essence of Young Creativity

In a time when expression and creativity shape the world we live in, it is vital to encourage and cherish the artistic endeavours of our future generations. Thus, we present to you "A Kaleidoscope of Poetic Whispers", an extraordinary collection of poems written by the talented students of Global Indian School. This anthology serves as a testament to their budding genius and speaks volumes about their unique perspectives and experiences. From personal stories to powerful social commentaries, this anthology delves deep into the rich tapestry of human experience through the lens of budding poets. The themes explored within these poems provide a remarkable insight into the lives and concerns of our students. Whether it is love, heartbreak, friendship, nature, identity, or injustice, each piece encapsulates a slice of their reality.

Poetry offers a path to self-expression, providing an outlet for the joys, struggles, and inner contemplations that shape our lives. These young poets have fearlessly embarked on this journey, bravely delving into the depths of their hearts and minds to expose their thoughts and feelings through verse. Moreover, this anthology is a testament to the supportive and nurturing environment Global Indian

School strives to create and the dedication of our teachers who have guided and inspired them along the way.

I take this opportunity to thank Deccan Imprints' unwavering commitment in nurturing creative talent. By publishing the anthology, "A Kaleidoscope of Poetic Whispers" you have provided our budding poets with a platform to share their voices and perspectives. I extend my heartfelt gratitude and admiration to all the students who have contributed their poetic masterpieces to this collection.

I am honoured to have been part of their journey as they navigate the realms of poetry. My hope is that this anthology will inspire others to unearth their creative talents, fuel their passion for self-expression, and recognize the profound impact that the written word can have on both the writer and the reader.

Dhaya Derek Philip
HOD, English Department

Dedicated. Smart. Fearless. Strong. Eager to change the world. Willing to pursue their passion. Those are just a few words that describe some of the Global Indian School students you will meet in the pages of this issue. As my team and I put together the poems and short stories we were ecstatic to see such beautifully penned thoughts and I would like to appreciate all these young minds for expressing their perception in such an articulate manner.

Is it a millennial thing that attracts these young minds to such conviction? Is it just that we've become such a global society that they can't help but be more aware of the needs of humans worldwide through freedom of speech? Is it simply the idealism of youth?

Regardless, our students share a common passion of translating their passion and emotions into words of wisdom.

We are delighted to be a part of the event and look forward to many more such opportunities.

I would like to thank Deccan Imprints for giving our students a platform to express their views and my team for bringing this together.

Best regards,

Janapriya B
Activity Coordinator (Gr 6-12)

As William Wordsworth once said, "Poetry is a spontaneous overflow of powerful feelings: it takes its origin from emotions collected in tranquility." The power of imagination and creativity knows no age limits. It is awe-inspiring to witness young minds of Global Indian School harnessing their unique perspectives and pouring them into captivating poetries.

In an era dominated by screens and instant gratification, the art of writing seems to have taken a backseat. However, these young poets have defied the norm by embracing their passion as a means of expression. Through their poems, they remind us of the beauty inherent in literature and its power to change lives. They challenge us to see beyond the distractions of the digital age and reconnect with the joy of reading, igniting a passion that may have been dormant within us.

We are filled with immense joy for being presented with such an opportunity, looking forward to more.

Sincerely,

Anooja Nair
Student Editor (Gr 11-A- Science)

CONTENTS

1. Ages of love

Anooja Nair
11-A (science)

I was born free to love and hate,
And I choose love and that was my biggest mistake.
Different faces and different sights,
Made me insecure of my life.
I have ignored the bad and the good,
But love, was something I never understood.

It was like a magical book,
That I had to take a look.
As sweet as it sounds,
Sour, evil and jealously are its compounds.
My body had once drowned in that book,
Which became the talk of the town.

Hours of talking under the moon,
Past afternoon, in the month of June.
Now I sit in the rocky chair,
Smoking a pack of cigarette.
The memories are too painful to forget,
Full of regrets.

Now I have become a tired old man,
Sick of love and sick of life.
Sick of people around me,
Who march through my head all day.
A man is never sincere in life,
He doesn't know to love and only has pride.

One day when he loses his pride,
The world will turn away except his black silhouette.

2. My white lady and Chandrayan-3

Aastha Varshney

8-B

The moon I saw in rhymes and childhood dreams,
Shimmering and silver with a frail rounded
appearance, I watched and watched it with awe on
many nights,
With my silver and white colors,
I drew in my drawing books.
The moon that seemed serene and poised,
made me sit and reflect on many nights.
Oh! My fair lady, you were in the heavens
unreachable, unattainable.
Yet the same moon looked forlorn and rugged…..
When the Chandrayan-3 landed.
Where was your beauty I had savored for years?
Are you sad and lost my dear lady…
away from us, far away?
Do not be lonely, my dear beauty;
we have reached you finally,
Facing the challenges and the perils.
Do rest, my graceful lady …
n our warm and loving arms.

3. Silent Spring

Abel Paul Nilayattingal
6-E

No birds twittering,
Only chainsaws buzzing in the silent spring.

No monkeys are flinging from branch to branch, Only
snares to catch them and trap.

The river is toxic, the fish are dead, The
animals who drink only see red.

No one can bear the animal's plight, So
why aren't they helping them fight?

The answer is clear; no one wants to spend for them, Lest
their money starts to end.

The animals precious forest is done,
Unless somebody wants to spend,

Their life and worth just for them.

4. Anxiety's Maze

Adila Navas
11-A (Science)

Anxiety's whisper, a constant hinder
Heartbeats like thunder, thoughts like a storm,
Invisible struggles, emotions unsure

Restless nights, tangled in racing thoughts,
A weight on the chest, a burden to bear.
But in the struggle a warrior rose,
Finding strength from depth within

A battle within, where courage must rise,
Fighting myself, seeking clear skies
Through the games of anxiety's maze,

In the midst of chaos, I found peace within.
A way to heal and ease my mind,

Though the road is long and unsure
The warrior in me is still potent
With hope as my guide, I carry the light,
Marching through the maze,
Harnessing my inner might.

5. IN MY SLEEP

Devananda Suresh
8-C

In my sleep I close my eyes,
for the next day I've got to rise.
In my sleep I drift off far,
to the land of magic with chocolate bars.
In my sleep, I've got to see,
 The whelm of the beautiful mermaid seas.
In my sleep I saw nearby,
A princess here and a fairy in the sky.
In my sleep I love to dream,
for it brought me happiness's beam.
I'd love to dream all over again,
but I don't like dreams with fighting men.
Why do I dream, I wonder why?
But my answers are incorrect my brain simply cries.

6. Curse of Emptiness
Khadeeja Liba
9-B

Emptiness is to be a body without a soul
It deprives everything of its beauty.
What beauty is to see without love?
What beauty is the dark sea without stains
of the moon loomed over it?
What beauty is death without its sorrow?
To be empty is the curse of prometheus,
To be chained to the torment of immortality.
Where there's no honourable death,
no mercurial finale,
just a plagued series of remaining.

7. The forget-me-nots, 1939

Rida Harris

12-B

Tears streamed across my face
Though I knew that I could not cease this
I wailed and wailed
Hoping that he wouldn't descend the stairs
Hoping that he wouldn't leave me solus.

Yet he avowed that he would return
 And handed me his cherished forget-me-nots saplings
 Before giving his word that he would return
Before the saplings grew lush and green.

As years rolled away, the forget-me-nots
grew beside me.
The cycle of seasons passed sustained from
Awakening Springs to Brisk winters
Flowers grew and withered away Yet,
I saw no sight of him.

Upon entering papa's room,
Years of locked away memories greeted me
I recalled the time, he said I should be like him
A patriotic, man-at-arms like him.

At another dawn, I was greeted by a sight
Which I longed to see for years
Before the forget-me-nots withered away
There came my father
Bearing something more than victory.

Years shot up like my maturity and I
Became what was intended for me,
Awaiting to handover my share of forget-me-nots.

8. Echoes of Creativity

Muhammed Aman

7-C

In pages filled with ink and dreams,
A world of wonder brightly gleams.
"My School My Book," a journey starts,
Where youthful voices paint their arts.

Short stories woven, tales unfold,
In words and phrases, young minds mold.
Imagination takes its flight,
Guided by the day and night.

Poems dance with rhythm and rhyme,
Echoing thoughts in every line.
"My School My Book," an open door,
To share what's felt, and so much more.

In classrooms' echo, friendships bloom,
In shared stories, there's ample room.
A tapestry of voices strong,
United in the tales they throng.

Oh, let the pages come alive,
With tales from hearts that dare to strive.
"My School My Book," a legacy,
Where words inspire, forever free.

Submit your pieces, let them soar,
To realms unknown, to worlds explore.
With pen in hand and hearts ablaze,
We write our stories, voices raise.

"My School My Book," an ode to us,
A legacy that's bound to last.
With every word, a mark we leave,
In pages turned, our dreams conceive.

So take a step, unleash your art,
For in these pages, souls impart.
"My School My Book," a canvas wide,
Where creativity turns the tide.

Embrace the pen, the paper's kiss,
Create a world that's purest bliss.
In every tale, in every rhyme,
Our voices echo for all time.

9. Snow flakes

Bhadra Sudeer
9-C

Snowflakes fall one by one,
And float away one by one.
I really miss you.
If I had been a snowflake,
I would have reached you sooner.
So that I can see you,
So that I can meet you,
I really miss you!

10. MOM

Fathima Faisel
11-A (Science)

Who ran to me when I fell,
with all her love and care.
I felt her pain more than mine,
her scolds full of agonized glare.
All these things that make me raged,
Are more than precious once it's past.
Once again when it's revived,
I neglect my precious mind.
But as it passes and goes on,
I have a box filled with memories,
Precious than my life.

11. A Slumber did my spirit seal

Hiba Fatma

9-A

A slumber did my spirit seal
I had no human fears.
She seemed a thing that could not feel,
The touch of every years.

No motion has she now, no force
She neither hears or sees.
Rolled round in earth's diurnal course,
With rocks, and stones and trees

12. For the first time in my life

Krishna Priya Suresh

9-A

For the first time in my life,
I climbed the stairs to sky.
Empire grown so tall,
I caught the land in my heart.
For the first time in my life,
Saw the peaks in a frame.
Felt like I could fall any minute
The future is unknown
But now it's grown so far.

13. A Bitter-Sweet Tale Of a Lover's Grief

Manal Zubair
9-C

In euphoric dreams, he resides,
A lover's tale, where reality collides.
Clinging to merry memories of old,
A story of love that time couldn't hold.

He walks the streets with an empty chair,
His wife, he pretends, is always there.
He dines alone at their favorite place,
Conversing softly, a smile on his face.

In their cherished café, he dines alone,
Ordering for two, his love for her shown.
He speaks to her, though she can't reply,
A love so deep, it won't ever die.

He whispers his secrets, his hopes, his fears,
Invisible presence, to wipe his tears.
In his world of make-believe, they remain,
A bittersweet tale of love's enduring reign.

14. A BOTANICAL BALLAD

Silpa Shajan
12-A (Science)

One fine day the romantic rose
Scented sweet for the lovely lilly

Lilly lover, the ominous orchid
cried to the cantankerous corpse Confine they did,
the romantic rose in the pernicious pitcher

Rational rosy thorns Pierced
the pitcher Lovely Lilly shone
Blushed with bleeding hearts

One fine day the ostentatious orchid
 Fell for the fairy duster

Fairy lover, the cantankerous corpse
Punched him with his pungent!

15. FLOWERS

Sreenanda Sandhya
10-A

I like flowers.

I wouldn't like t o receive them, however.

They all go rotten in a few months or weeks
Although t hey look nice and smell sweet
I used to admire flowers

I even had some favorite ones, moreover.

But I don't think I'll ever want a bouquet again.
And any ot her, I'll refrain
Beca use if the las t 3 bouquets were corrupted,
Why would another one be trusted?

It 's only natural for a bouquet to be dried
But can't you see I tried?
How I kept them in a china vase

Filled it up with water, and took care of it for days?
Maybe it didn't get t he r ight t ype of care
I guess flowers are never fair.

16. PREPARED

Zareen Sheikh

11-B

Sometimes, you just need to keep believing.
You have what it takes
You ain't making mistakes
You have already the built the pace,
You just need some space.
Why do you worry?
You don't need to hurry
You're all prepared.

17. The earnings of life

Anooja Nair
11-A (Science)

I get respect when I work well,
Trapped inside a door less shell.
My earnings are always important,
As I feel my life has shortened.
As my income goes higher and higher.
I start to dream and desire.
My heart burning like a fire,
Weird sounds through my head like choir.
My soul throbbing with throes,
Knowing that my end is close.
I feeling that I ought to a propose,
My feelings have froze.
My head aching from the bawling,
I had to save myself and my belongings.
Going on and on exploring,
My life is on the line that someone is calling.
An eye speaking a million lies,
It is me who I am going to prioritize.
Everyday feels like a Monday,
Where originality has stunned me.
Everybody judges me based on my money,
But nobody knows I am lonely.

18.   Is This Where I Truly Belong?

Adila Navas

11-A (Science)

In solitude's caress, I find my quiet place,
Where thoughts can dance, and time slows its pace.
Amidst the hush of wordly play,
I ask myself, "Is this where I truly belong today?"

Lost in a world where inconsistency is praised
I seek my place, where life's purpose is raised
Amidst the hush of wordly play,
I hopped on a journey, free from flight.

A journey unfolds, unburdened by flight,
A quest to find the layers of me
Embracing flaws and strengths to thrive ,
Revisiting my story, where I come alive.

I retraced my story ,Oh who is to complain
They're part of me, an irregular whole,
A masterpiece of imperfections and hope
Unveiling the grace beneath the lies,
I claimed myself no longer confined

Amidst the hush of wordly play,
I became my storyteller, a poet unchained.
On the quest for answers, I'm my own guide,

Discovering that belonging is a feeling of heart
And not a place where I'm forced
I found myself nestled within my heart
Where I've been all along.

19. ALONE IN DARK

Fathima Faisel
11-A (Science)

I walked to my room with a candle lit.
I sat down by the pane, and wished to be gay.
I felt so lonely,
with each passing second.
I heard the rustling leaves, so,
mourning as can ever be.
I sobered in the creepy hush,
as the wind whispered to me.
I felt puzzled by the mystery,
that it shared a cold tremble past me.
I breathed a deep sigh, as I longed for a chat.
I was left alone in utter, with a company of four,
I, me, the candle and myself.

20. STORY ABOUT THE RAIN

Krishna Priya Suresh
9C

They live as a family Together all over the world
Not a single place
Where they don't have a house.

There was a little one with them.
After the summer he cried so bad
For the toy he lost that summer.
During the summer no one could cry
It was a rule in their family .
He was not alone cause his family joined him ,
They've been holding their tears for long
Their tears came down As what we call the rain"
Said little boy who Made a story of rain.

21. Love's Eternal Embrace

Manal Zubair

9-C

In a cozy home where love does bloom,
A husband and wife, sharing the same room.
Hand in hand, they stride through life's way,
Two souls entwined, come what may.

Through laughter, tears, they journey along,
A love so deep, like a bird's first song.
In morning's embrace, in evening's peace,
Their bond strengthens, never to cease.

Dancing through life, a sway so sweet,
Love's tale etched in each heartbeat.
Listening, smiling, in a sacred place,
An unbroken bond, a warm embrace.

Yet when the sun sets beyond the view,
Truth emerges, stark and true.
In dusk silence, the reality unfurls,
Her spirit departed from this world.

Invisible yet present, a love that's pure,
Enduring beyond time, forever secure.
A man and memories forever combined,
Love lives on, in his heart enshrined.

22. Did she deserve it?

Zareen Sheikh
11-B (Commerce)

Once upon a time there lived a happy girl,
Who got traumatized afterwards.
She became comfy crying Drowned herself,
In a pool of red tears Hiding all her fears
She lost hope because of it,
Did she deserve all of it?

23. My best friend

Anooja Nair
11-A (Science)

You're my strength and support,
You're my one and only hope.
It's with you I want to spend my life,
It's with you where my love resides.
You always help me when I feel broke,
Always going to be my first hero.
Learning life lessons in a nice way,
As I am travelling around life's highway.
You're the greatest human that I have ever met,
As my world revolves around this nest.
You're the emotion I feel at night,
You're arms spread out to keep me warm.
I will forever miss you,
Once I end this drastic life.
When I used to procrastinate,
You made me feel like the best candidate.
You held my hands strong and steady,
Never did you let go of me.
I see how our relation has changed,
Never will it be rearranged.
Growing older together made me feel good,
You know exactly when I am misunderstood.
Sweet, sour and strong like heather,
Thank you for your unconditional love my mother!

24. GREEN LAND'S GRAINS

Silpa Shajan
12-A (Science)

Revolutionaries of the green Come as a bunch
To save your rights Why to beg
When there aren't empty barns.
May the kingdom rise up
With all might
Not for a war, but for its pride
and people Let the soil refine
For the goodness of crops and people.
Why to beg the monsoon
When the science of crops Is in our hands.
May the kingdom rise up With all might
To fill the empty tummies of thousands
Let the green flourish
For the greatness of India

25. SHADES OF LIFE

Fathima Faisel
11-A (Science)

Life in joy is like a river,
forever fresh and flowing.
Once miserable is like a sea,
slowly tearing up by the shore.
Upon pique, it turns into a body
bubbling in wrath and heat.
Being alone its an ocean
clear, pure and serene.
These distinct shades of life,
painted in colors, vivid and bright
all blend in my face, leaving
a smile, neither true nor false
just a blank one, faint but divine.

26. Illusion

Zareen Sheikh
11-B (Commerce)

At times, we feel like we're nothing,
We just want to be someone
I know it's hard, But keep going on.
We try our best every time
But nothing seems to be right
 But you don't just give up now
You have come this far.
You need to wake up from this bad dream
You need to be more keen
Or you'll end up achieving,
Nothing that you dream.
We feel like giving up,
But we all want to win it
The truth is,
Life is an illusion

27. The trip to heaven

Anooja Nair
Gr. 11-A (Sceince)

I never thought twice before ending my life,
Stabbing myself with a painful knife.
Looking back at my dark days,
No one had hurt me neither did they stay.
My emotions taking control over me,
I wish to be free.
Those negative talks surrounding my head,
Not wanting to go ahead.
My muscles starting to feel numb,
Forgetting who I want to become.
My breathe getting unsteady,
Is this my end already?
Stopping myself from being pity,
Saying goodbye to this lovely city.
Warm blood slipped out my chest,
I had to go through this life test.
Colorful days have come to an end,
Now I don't have to pretend.
All I ever needed was a true friend,
Someone who I could depend.

28. BELOVED STRANGER

Fathima Faisal
11-A (Science)

I have lost myself,
to some stranger I just met.
Even his blankest of stares
went piercing into my heart.
His voice began echoing within myself
 Captivating my vagrant soul.
Stealing glances at him has enhanced
 to being my ardent addiction.
I have developed a passion for him
 that would certainly last a lifetime.
His journey through my life
 set off from being a stranger
and ceased to being my world.

29. Reborn

Anooja Nair
110A (Science)

My story is unsaid here,
The tension was severe.
Something burning inside me,
Is it fear?
I thought it was the first step after darkness,
My body aching from the sharpness.
Everyone surrounding me with questions,
Asking me if I learned my lesson.
My mom's glossy eyes filled with tears,
The one who truly cares.
I closed my eyes with frustration,
Wanting to be alone in this situation.
The head aching and my heart throbbing,
Within minutes I was sobbing.
I didn't want to live at all.
God gave me a second chance to recall.
I didn't want to breathe again,
My life not being a ten.
The white walls made me insane,
Not wanting to remember the pain.
As I have nothing to remain,
Despair and misery fills up my brain.

30. PROOF OF LOVE
FATHIMA FAISEL
GRADE: 11A (SCIENCE)

Having to prove one's love
 is a task as hideous as time.
No matter the trials or tests,
nor the time spent in attempts
It is a venture awaiting to
mock us with a gift of nothing.
Because love is a feeling,
so profound and boundless.

31. Love is back

ANOOJA NAIR
GRADE: 11A (SCIENCE)

It was my time recovering,
I was still discovering.
My neck was covered with a white cloth,
It was still hurting and unbearable.
Through the door of the four walls,
She swept through with a pace.
A simple red dress that swayed away.
Her hair was curly and she was so fair,
I was surprised to see her beauty, she was rare.
She came inside and smiled at me,
That just might be the start of 'we'.
As her hands touched my chest,
She knew I was depressed.
She was tall, pretty and lovely,
And before she left looked at me roughly.
Our eyes locked with an unconscious mind,
I knew at once that there was nothing else to hide.
I met her once again,
You know the thoughts of men.
Something is to be regretted,
Our heart was still embedded.
That night my mind was all on her,
Soon on my mind for years.

32. POWER OF WEAK

FATHIMA FAISEL
GRADE: 11a (SCIENCE)

We, deep within us, have the power
 to turn anything to its polar extreme.
There's always a way turn even a
cursed mishap into a celestial boon.
Nothing can stop us from achieving
what is rightfully ours.
Never think of anything as fatal.
We never know when an unfortunate blunder
 can be the cause of something ever better.

Never dishearten yourself
 for being weak at times.
Everyone in this world has their turn to shine.
Our weakness, then, won't be
an obstacle in the course of life.
Instead, the very same one day
 will prove to be more than worthy.

33. Missing spots
ANOOJA NAIR
GRADE: 11A (SCIENCE)

Some people in life are like diamonds,
Their value's high but no one notices.
Once they are gone we know their value,
It called the missing spots of a person.
People like us are insane in this world,
We deserve no love,
We have no fear.
People like us are hatred to this world,
Where none of us are kind,
Where none of us are sincere.
We do all things to please others,
Never have we done something to please the one who suffers.
We speak the lies like pure truth,
But god knows who to choose.
Sometimes we feel like a stoned figure,
As no one really care about our feelings.
Like our muscles have turned numb,
We have no other words to speak.
Most of our emotions are kept hidden,
But truth shall always be forbidden.

34. OUR STORY

FATHIMA FAISEL
GRADE: 11A (SCIENCE)

In the moon's glow, our story began,
God sent a gem, a perfect love plan.
But foolish and blind, I let it slip away,
Took it for granted day after day.

Regret filled my heart, like a naive teen,
Realized the beauty that could have been.
I yearned for another chance, a second start,
To hold them close, never to be apart.

Now, fate smiles upon us, in a twist of fate,
God reunited our hearts, it's never too late.
Like clumsy teens, we stumble,
and we learn, Cherishing every moment,
love's sweet return.

Under the moon's light, we hold hands tight,
Knowing now, love is worth the fight.
No longer an amateur, but wiser and strong,
Together we'll make melodies,
our hearts' sweet song.

35. The lost memories

ANOOJA NAIR
GRADE: 11A (SCIENCE)

It felt like a new beginning,
I have aimed straight to winning.
This is a game I cannot lose,
It is a decision I choose.
There are a few moments I wish to forget,
My problems disappear after a cigarette.
I have adopted many bad habits,
And now I wish to be wrapped in a blanket.
Removing bad memories with a tablet,
Doesn't help when you're being pulled like magnets.
Love is the best liar,
To feel misunderstood prior.
When silence is the only answer,
This becomes my only chance to romance her.
The days go by within a short amount of time,
And I feel like I'm committing a crime.
I want to secure what's mine,
A story that ends right in time.
My heart has begun to flutter,
I hope to be her only lover.
Keeping all hopes high,
Then comes the question 'why'?

36. OUR LOVE
FATHIMA FAISEL
GRADE: 11A (SCIENCE)

In a world of uncertainties,
you emerged like a radiant star,
Your love's touch, a soothing balm, healing all scars.
With humble gratitude,
I pour my heart out in rhyme,
For your unwavering devotion,
transcending space and time.

Through life's labyrinth,
you illuminate my way,
Each step emboldened by your love's warm ray.
Mountains may crumble and rivers may cease to flow,
But your love remains steadfast, a beacon aglow.

In your embrace, I find solace and peace,
A sanctuary where worries and fears cease.
With every breath, my heart sings your name,
Forever indebted to you, my love,
for igniting love's flame.

So here I stand, humbled by your affection's might,
Grateful for the gift of you, my eternal light.
In this symphony of love, forever we'll entwine,
Blessed by your unconditional love, eternally thine.

37. Roses

ANOOJA NAIR
GRADE: 11A (SCIENCE)

The red roses over the fence,
Carried beauty that was immense.
The color seems to make me gay,
Oh! The way they dance and sway.
The rosarium always made me smile,
Each feature was versatile.
The queen of flowers,
Made for lovers,
And all those people who loves themselves.
The symbol of love,
And the love that comes from above,
All makes up my day knowing I have somewhere to stay.
I realize that life is not full of roses,
Sometimes like a delphinium.
They define divine poetry,
As I look through the window quietly.
The sight shows me a sense of unity,
This makes me believe in humanity.
The beautiful red roses over the fence,
Gives me a desire which is intense.

38. WHY?
FATHIMA FAISEL
GRADE: 11A (SCIENCE)

The first encounter stranded me curious
Maybe cause you weren't cordial,
or perhaps I just didn't like you.
You were rude, frosty and sulky.
Your cold face made me uneasy.
I kept an eye on you every so often,
almost scanning for emotions
on your utterly barren profile.

You were unlike anyone I knew.
You were an absolute alien to me.
I didn't know what I wanted from you.
Didn't know what it meant to me.
My thoughts just won't go away.
The first time seeing you smile,
felt like a glimpse I was dying for.
For me it always was about you.
Prejudice turned to endearment.
We were never allies; we would've never been.
But in the end who cares anyway.
Wasn't it obvious I love you?

39. True dreams

ANOOJA NAIR
GRADE: 11A (SCIENCE)

The most prestige thing about me is my job,
A job I always wanted as a kid for which I used to sob.
It in a way is the reason for the respect I receive,
A respect I always deceived.
I met a lot of people during this journey,
Including a few people who would concern me.
The most fearful job ever,
But the happiness lasts forever.
I have never slept peacefully from that day,
The day my surgery delayed.
I took a few lives with me,
Do I deserve my degree?
The stencils that I carry with me,
Is used to cure many people, I guarantee.
There has always been a burning flame inside me,
My hands quiver and so as my knees.
To give people a peaceful life is my trait,
But what I receive more in abundance is hate.

40. ILLUSION
FATHIMA FAISEL
GRADE: 11A (SCIENCE)

I believe you are an illusion something
that my mind created for me to love and feel loved.
I keep fantasizing you in me,
with me in different stages of life.
Feeling of connection so mythical,
Desire is simply beyond description.
I can barely justify your existence in this dream
I'm floating in,
to realize all my fears and tears dissolve
in just your presence.

I cherish every moment with you.
In your eyes, I lose myself.
I feel at ease, even in silence
when our skin caresses each other.
I accept you with your past,
and love you in your present
in a way that lasts until our future.

41. A good reason

ANOOJA NAIR
GRADE 11A (SCIENCE)

The best effort is the best step,
And most importantly is help.
True love a person can share is wealth
 in this modern world,
People have become heartless and that's how
the world has turned.
A crazy man knows to love money,
To hate the one in need,
And to curse at the poor.
Tell me a good reason to be a nuisance.
Being selfish is the trend,
A game to disrespect our so-called friends.
A sign to be a good human,
Turned into an illusion.
The hate being passed on to the generations,
Has tortured and ruined all relations.
We should change all expectations,
Tell me a good reason to remove all frustrations.
The small world has gotten people crazy,
Simplicity has made me lazy.
The relation between love and hate is stupid,
Tell me a good reason to believe in cupid.

42. ATTIC
FATHIMA FAISEL
GRADE 11A SCIENCE

Somewhere in that house you see
Is a dark and musty, tiny room. Step-by-step,
ascend the stairs you'll come across a tiny door.
Locked and latched, tightly packed,
closed and sealed by a tiny lock.
A messy room, poorly lit, stuffed and
filled with tiny things.
It's might as well a massive house,
but I prefer the tiny space.
Here is where years ago,
I left myself, a tiny kid.
As of now, I'm an older me
and miss myself a tiny bit.
How perfect would my life have been,
If I'd just remain the tiny me.

43. A small wish
ANOOJA NAIR
GRADE 11A SCIENCE

Life has taught me many lessons,
And one was to keep my possessions.
I wish I could do everything right,
But everything ends up with a fight.
Am I just problematic?
Or is it just them being dramatic.
They say to treat a woman with respect,
Are they dumb thinking woman don't give us any affect.
For all my spontaneous wishes,
I thank my mom for her support and kisses.
Going through insomnia is definitely not fine,
But staying away from drama is divine.
I grew up as a child with numerous wishes,
Who learned to imagine and to respect the riches.
Growing up my wishes have changed,
As event in life has been rearranged.
Prayers help to change our fate they say,
Nothing helps when you're born this way.
Hold people close to your heart they say,
All I do is to push people away.

44. END
FATHIMA FAISEL
GRADE 11A SCIENCE

If a moment is to come when my pen runs dry.
The only reason is
my eyes whom I let to cry.
For something that I did unconditionally rely.
For someone whose face I still search up in the sky.

45. A perfect human

ANOOJA NAIR

I am not the person I used to be,
My wings are out and they wish to be free.
I have never called myself a human as I am greedy,
Life towards success is never going to be easy.
I needed hard work to grow and develop,
I have never put someone down to step up.
If humans don't support each other,
Life is going to be played by a theatre.
If the world is only going to have morose,
Our life will turn into a joke.
Memories are to be stuck together,
Where our moments turn into heather.
I have always tried to live without any issues,
But problems in my life seem to continue.
I don't really know where to start,
But all the love comes from my heart.

46. DEAR TEACHER
FATHIMA FAISEL
GRADE 11A SCIENCE

Heeding certain experiences in life,
I made errors, more than one or two.
I lost hope, patience and my soul,
Yet you alone stayed by me like a dew.
Your aura was the strength
I needed to deal the misery I went through.
Your smile let out an enchanted
spell like that of a mysterious sorceress.
The warmth of love and safety
I felt Can be gifted by none other than you.
It is indeed the least I could do,
to let you know the pain I feel,
as my time with you has ceased.
May you never forget me or
the time you shared with me.
I'll end my quote, with a tiny note.
For all that you've done my dear teacher.
I'd thank you and thank you again.

47. Nightmares

ANOOJA NAIR
GRADE 11A SCIENCE

The glass shattered into pieces,
It is my heart beat that increases.
My dad pushed my mom over,
I knew that he was not sober.
He looked at me angrily and then at mom,
I saw my mom trying to stay calm.
He walked over and asked me for the keys,
I sat in the corner hugging my knees.
'I don't have it' I said quietly,
His eyes burning like fire.
My mom was shivering,
Even I was quivering.
He held my mom by her neck,
He surely had a great effect.
My mom trying her best to catch breath,
I immediately pushed him as mom was close to death.
Such nightmares started to occur in my head,
I don't really know what is waiting ahead.

48. THE HEART

FATHIMA FAISEL
GRADE 11A SCIENCE

God blessed us, mortals, with an ever-so-funny muscle.
It beats against our chest but never breaks free.
It resides within us, yet beats for another being.
Its delight knows no limit on the sight of its dear one.
It holds within a fiery desire for love,
hope and dreams.
It slowly dies as the fire fades,
and evolves into an eternal frame.
For all the people it had held
to cherish forever and beyond.

49. LOVE-WRECK

Fathima Faisel
11-A Science

A farce smile veils her grief caused
by her love lost so long.
Her tears with a glimpse of herself embraced in past.
Scenes of quite delight flashes through her dreams.
Alas! She had to witness the sight of her
only love drowning to doom.
Surely, she knows, for the man
she loves is never to return.
She feels him in her every breath,
as it was his gift to her.
He slowly froze to death content in saving his love.
She rose as the sun at dawn,
with only his memories
and his warmest of smiles.

50. Nights of despair

ANOOJA NAIR
GRADE 11A SCIENCE

Every night was filled with despair,
Of memories I could never repair.
Being lonely at home was fine,
But feelings were crossing the line.
I wanted someone to share life with,
But people always dare to snitch.
Not everyone is of the same kind,
God makes sure that there is a job assigned.
Not everyone is of the pure mind,
Most people cheat on the blind.
I was once in that stage,
Thinking of it brings me rage.
I wish I had someone to have deep conversations,
But they all are not up to my expectations.
I might be a bit demanding,
But I hope they became a bit more understanding.

51. Love like lemons
ANOOJA NAIR
GRADE 11A SCIENCE

As sour as a lemon,
Is another world called heavens.
My love as sweet as lemons,
Soon had turn to life lessons.
I tried my best to give her the best impression,
I treated her like my own possession.
Maybe, that is where I went wrong,
But I had to stay strong.
I really hope it is not my fault,
As our love story became like salt.
My mind is trying to stay calm,
I don't want to cause her any harm.
Maybe it is my possessive behavior which gave her off,
She left me stranded with a scoff.
I wish I wasn't too harsh on her,
I knew she endured my pain for years.
Our love was really like lemons,
Sour at first but memories fresher than ever.

52. BLUE
ANOOJA NAIR
GRADE 11A SCIENCE

My favorite color is blue,
It always expresses what I'm going through.
It is the color of blueberries,
It tells me my actions are to be worried.
It is not just a color but a true feeling,
That has a very deep meaning.
The blue sky over me,
Gives me a sense of relief.
Not all shades are sad,
It is the reputation that is bad.
The ocean is blue as well as the sky,
They make me dream so high.
I don't know if it is all true,
I'll do anything to be back with you.
My feelings have turned blue,
Let's turn this love into something new.
I am that silly kind of blue,
What type of blue are you?

53. Growing older
ANOOJA NAIR
GRADE 11A SCIENCE

Step by step we learn about things,
Day by day we fly with our wings.
Not everything we do is right,
But that is how we reach good height.
Skipping up homework seemed to be fun,
But solving life problems could never be undone.
Dreaming was a part of growing,
And they become true without us knowing.
My life has always been a wild game,
Through it came all the shame.
I really regret what I have done,
More problems appear, from which I run.
Life was much easier back then,
I hope to live through that time again.
With new problems coming and old ones still staying,
All I am doing now is praying.
Inch-by-inch, day-by-day,
I am getting close to god.
I hope things get better,
As I can't handle this pressure.

54. Birthdays

ANOOJA NAIR
GRADE 11A SCIENCE

The time of the year when you get excited,
Also the time when you feel devastated.
If cutting the birthday cake alone is bad,
Then that makes me glad.
I am used to these types of days,
Sadness in many different ways.
To all the people who love me,
Sorry, I don't accept things for free.
To all the people I love,
Sorry, the real love is for the one above.
I don't wish for a birthday gift,
Just keep the relationship we have built.
Being selfish is my trait I admit,
And there is nothing about me that you can predict.
That one candle on my cake,
Is the only reason why I am awake.
There is no wish I make on this day,
But I wish my mom would come back awake.
Even on this happy day,
I lie to myself that I am ok.

55. Night-time

ANOOJA NAIR
GRADE 11A SCIENCE

When the night falls,
I see myself looking over to the moon.
I see the stars shinning for me,
I see the wind waving at me.
I find myself amused by everything,
The night surely has a great power.
It has the power to keep everyone quiet,
It has the power to keep me fascinated.
But I wish it could be more understanding,
I wish it could solve my problems.
I am soft human being,
God, please love me.
Like the moon that changes shapes,
I wish to take my moods away.
I wish to be free like the stars,
That shines bright in the sky.
I wish to be the owl of the night,
That watches and learns everything quietly.
I wish my life was as peaceful as the night,
I wish to know what is right.

56. Numbness

ANOOJA NAIR
GRADE 11A SCIENCE

I hate to admit the truth,
When all you gave me was wonders.
Because of you I ruined my youth,
My life flashed before my eyes like thunders.
It really must be destiny,
To not be loved.
It was my wealth and money,
That was your beloved.
The person who used to run my mind,
Is the person I hate the most.
To the life I left behind,
I feel stabbed by the throat.
I thought you were different,
But the snakes don't change.
You made my life difficult,
Now I'm left with rage.
I should have known the consequences,
Before I fell into the well.
You gave me all kind of stresses,
But something's are personnel.

57. Backseat driver
ANOOJA NAIR
GRADE 11A SCIENCE

You pushed me out of your life like a paper,
I never knew what should be done at that moment.
I tried to get you back many times,
But all my efforts seem useless.
Now the question is, do you deserve me?
The question that makes me sleepless.
Even if I loved you back then,
The love seems to be fading.
We both were young back then,
And mistakes were common.
But such a mistake should not be done,
That is inerasable.
I hope to see you back in your senses,
I hope you understand your loss.
I won't blame you for the past,
As the revenge is kept for the future.
I have never betrayed anyone,
And thus I know who will win.
I hope your pride puts you down,
You carry more poison that a venom.
I hope you try to understand,
It's hard for me too.
I feel like a backseat driver.

58. After party

ANOOJA NAIR
GRADE 11A SCIENCE

I remember the time I had to clean up,
There were paper cups all over.
The mess was too much to handle,
I didn't know what to do.
The house was a complete mess,
One of my bulbs had broken,
I was starting to sweat as I had office in an hour.
The party took a long time,
And everyone was drunk,
I had to get them to their respective partners.
With a few heels and hearts broken,
I cleaned the place up into a heaven.
I wanted to sleep very badly,
But I rather clean this mess.
I was also drunk,
But being sober didn't really help.
Today had me going crazy,
But being alone forever could have me dead.

59. The letter D

ANOOJA NAIR
GRADE 11A SCIENCE

The most beautiful flowers are the daisies,
That looks at me with different gazes.
In different colors like different dishes,
It fills my heart with kisses.
When I'm worked up on my desk,
Trying to pay all the cheques,
I know that I'm slowly falling into darkness.
All I can do is scream and shout without any doubts.

60. MY DREAMLAND
FATHIMA FAISEL
GRADE 11A SCIENCE

I am in search of a place,
that I'll keep for myself.
A piece of earth unknown to men,
that hides even from the flying flocks.
Some place to conceal myself
from the crowds of the world.
Someplace where there's no one to judge me
and my thoughts.
A place to let all my dreams
grow wings of their own.
A place where I can let my wildest
of dreams come true.
Such a place that resides deep down within myself.
And right at that moment
when I find my very own land,
I'll call it, my dreamland.

61. Black pepper

ANOOJA NAIR
GRADE 11A SCIENCE

My life is just as black pepper,
Spicy and smoky with all the bad traits.
I always loved them,
Maybe as it represents my life.
One thing for sure is that I'd burn my mouth.
I don't want a long debate,
But peppers really make my day.
I don't know where to start,
But I hope things change fast.
Like the spicy peppers,
I wish time goes by fast,
As the taste would not last long.
Just like my crazy life,
I needed the crazy black peppers too!

62. My sister

ANOOJA NAIR
GRADE 11A SCIENCE

She is my best friend and my best enemy,
And talking with her kills me mentally.
She is my motivation and my strength,
Our relationship is very complex.
She never raised her hands on me,
But I always leave a bruise on her body.
With her by my side things are easy,
And without her I feel empty.
She is the only person who makes me smile,
Her behavior is really versatile.
She brings the best out of me,
She treats me like a VIP.
Her beauty is to be admired,
She takes it after my mother.
Everyone loves her,
She has been the queen for all these years.
She always makes me jealous,
She is just too precious.
Her life makes me hate myself,
As in front of her my problems are deaf.

63. Game

ANOOJA NAIR
GRADE 11A SCIENCE

You can change the game,
But don't let the game change you.
Remember that a human has nothing to lose,
But one or the other to gain and still they rise.
Wanting to be someone else,
Is a pure waste of time.
Instead we should try to be a rainbow,
In someone's life.
Not all of us have a healthy life,
But try to get the sunrise.
Not everybody can live happily,
So trust yourself when needed.
Don't be so sly,
It will never give you a living.
Remember to stay calm,
As the game your playing has no ending.

64. BROKEN!
FATHIMA FAISEL
GRADE 11A SCIENCE

Oh! Would you know?
When it is a heart that screams
at the forced demise of a bond.
A pair of eyes that refrains truth.
Truth - an embittered word for her since.
Echoing cracks heard by none in space.
Emotionally fragile, staring while he leaves stepping
on the broken pieces of glass.
Shaking breaths, insensate limbs partnered
with twin weary eyes.
Dim lights, glass shards and amidst a lone,
broken maiden.
Oh! Would you know?
If to be pronounced living henceforth,
for she's no more than a breathing corse.

65. Love with no limit
ANOOJA NAIR
GRADE 11A SCIENCE

From what I have learnt,
Love has no limit.
You can love anyone,
But make sure that it is from the heart.
Staying true is what you should learn,
As it can really hurt a person.
Even if you're dead inside,
Don't leave the love hanging.
Love can never bear to be left alone.
Love is sweeter than sugar,
Love is brighter than the sun.
Don't judge love from the starting,
Unless you want to be done.
Love has no limit,
And grace has no measure.
Power has no boundary,
But it sure is real.
Never question love as it can kill you,
Whereas, feeling love is the best emotion ever.

66. Windows

ANOOJA NAIR
GRADE 11A SCIENCE

If our mind was like a window,
We could look into them.
All of our thoughts will be out,
And sins will begin.
It would be a time where we can't hide anything,
And that is the beginning.
Our mind is very strong to withstand anything,
It all begins there.
If you try to ignore your conscience,
You won't live for long.
I spent many years inside this small window,
And experienced things which were horrible.
Make sure to not hurt yourself,
And windows have sharp corners.
Never lie to your mind,
As window can open and
look through them at night.
I wish that our minds were like windows,
So that when they shattered
we could change their panes.

67. What if I die?

ANOOJA NAIR
GRADE 11A SCIENCE

What if I die?
Will someone cry for me?
Will someone care for me?
I wonder how it is going to be.
I hope that I survive long enough,
As I still have dreams to fulfill.
Even in my death bed I will stay strong.
The only person I have is me.
To all the people who loved me in the past,
I genuinely thank from the bottom of my heart.
I hope I go to hell,
As most things I have done is cruel.
I hope god tortures me a lot,
So I know how to live in my future life.
Thinking about all the moments bring tears to my eyes,
I wish they were not true.
Being in this old form I thank,
Everyone who cared for me till now.
I hope I don't get emotional,
But everything in my life is sensational.

68. Time

ANOOJA NAIR
GRADE 11-A SCIENCE

Time never waits for anyone,
But in this game I have already won.
I always wanted love,
And received it immensely from the one above.
We can never predict the time,
As all it does is cover the crime.
Everything happens for a reason,
Now, just might not be your season.
But never blame time,
As it helps you regardless of its prime.
When you lie on your deathbed,
Remember the blood color is still red.
Humans should never go against each other,
If so, your life will turn into a theatre.
The more it goes,
The more it takes away.

69. God

ANOOJA NAIR
GRADE 11-A SCIENCE

God is the almighty,
He is the creator of all.
Doesn't matter how bad I may be,
All my wishes are recalled.
He makes magic work,
He makes us believe in dreams.
Even when we are overworked,
He still pushes us to the extreme.
There is nothing he can't solve,
It is in his presence we grow up.
He is the only one involved,
In getting our dreams woken up.
Never lose faith,
As it is something we can never replace.
The fear must always be there,
As god lives through all these days.
For god is always faithful,
His grace never ends.
Make sure that you pray,
Then, he will show you the right way.
He makes sure that we are aware,
To be honest he slays every day.

70. Days of Drummer
ANOOJA NAIR
GRADE 11A SCIENCE

He went away- away with the sea,
He smashed across the wind of the movie.
The raised up waves seems to bother
the boat he fiddled upon the days.

Looks on the eyes were contemplated,
with muscular brawny skin,
He lived across the yard of the filthy cook-witch.
The boat seems rusty with a tint of black scars,
He held the boat with prejudice that can't relate.

Boat kept its wave length not measuring the surface,
It made the whole set dark and a scene of mist.
This really seem to set off an award of bizarre,
It showed how mighty he was to let it
slid on like whirl on prick and throne.

71. Peer Pressure

ANOOJA NAIR
GRADE 11A SCIENCE

Sometimes it's hard to know the right,
But I still assure myself to the might.
I want to be seen out of sight,
I cry myself at night.

Words sound differently in my head,
I'm not over them yet.
It's like my soul is dead,
The pressure is too much to be said.
Im on my edge,
Not knowing my best.
Is it just me or everybody else?

72. Stupidness

ANOOJA NAIR
GRADE 11A SCIENCE

A man is very weak at heart,
He does not know that life is an art.
It has to be played smart,
A game of darts.
Time does not wait for him,
Recited like a beautiful hymn.
A never ending film,
A sudden whim.
He turns around for different ways,
Each moment was just a phase.
Only true friends stay,
Rest all are the unwanted preys.
He feels uncomfortable within the gaze,
Looks afar to escape the maze.
His life has a message that conveys,
One single soul, one displays.
A bit of might that takes him to say,
God is love, and no one ignores.
God is right, and no one opposes.
Truth that has been said before,
Became a lie in a man's throat.

73. Victor

ANOOJA NAIR
GRADE 11A SCIENCE

The paddy fields across my house,
Where I jumped up and down,
Brings me nostalgia.
The long, thin leaves,
The muddy ground, on a sunny week.
Sun blazing through my face,
Squinted eyes that I used to make.
We would go early in the morning,
And come back at dawn.
Our clothes dirty from the soft sordid ground.
My mom used to rebuke and thrash me,
But could never compensative for the mess I made.
My little feet all covered in mud,
Made my day a living bliss.
We took baths at the pond nearby,
Catching all the small fishes.
Smiling through the sorrows,
Going back all singing old hymns.

74. The old love

ANOOJA NAIR
GRADE 11A SCIENCE

Walking through the aisle,
Seeing many sights.
The calmest atmosphere alive,
A world I despise.
Flipping through the pages,
Characters feel alive.
Surrounded by surreal beauty,
A world I despise.
The sounds are louder in my heads,
I'm getting close to feeling it.
The meaning being stuck in my head,
The most adventurous life ahead.
I wish to be inside a book,
That has been written and not controlled.
Having a fixed destination gives me hope for the future end.
The prettiest heart around and the prettiest voice being told,
A person who has loved and hurt,
Might not know to love again.

75. A mistake
ANOOJA NAIR
GRADE 11A SCIENCE

Life became a sin after what I did,
My actions were discovered,
Within a speed of light.
I broke my trust over everything for her,
My vows were declined and those roses in bed.
I missed her touches and warm scent,
I missed those little hugs on my wasted days.
I missed those cherry cheeks that blushed after every compliment,
But definitely not those silly fights over someone else.
I got tired of the questions she would ask,
I got tired of saying those same three words over and over again.
I got tired of faking it till the very end.
And it all stopped when she left me for someone else.
It explains why being single is the best.
One to love and no one to tell.
Born alone, die alone.
Why do humans need someone else?

76. Flowers that go down

ANOOJA NAIR
GRADE 11A SCIENCE

Those little flowers that go down,
Even the spring seems to frown.
The grassy meadows are off to another land,
Wished I never took it for grand.
The air seemed to be dry,
I stood there leaving a huge sigh.
I wanted to go out to the sun,
And have fun of the things to the fullest.
The shiny sun standing tall,
But I cannot go out until fall.
Imagine running around the park,
Playing late till 6 o'clock.
The ice cream truck stands there torn out,
I wish to eat the ice-creams I adore.
When my mom leaves the room,
I would jump up and down with gloom.
But now look how it all has changed.
How the sun changes costume,
And my homework waits,
For sure I am doomed.
I wish at the end of June,
It finally arrives my new cartoon.

77. MIGHTIER THAN EVER
ANOOJA NAIR
GRADE 11A SCIENCE

Even bits of seeds desire,
a farmer's warmth and care is what they require.
A Farmer I met,
It was a total honour for me.

They work the best they can,
But don't get paid enough.
Their sweat often goes unnoticed.
Rain or heat they don't even care,
They work and work like no one can.
Their work is no joke,
A big salute to the milestones they achieve.

78. I CHOOSE KINDNESS
ANOOJA NAIR
GRADE 11A SCIENCE

Barriers broken down,
No one knew what it meant.
Discovering pieces of moments together,
Helping those with sincerity.
This kindness is meant.
It grows in heart,
Where the whole journey starts.
Look back from where you came,
It is no game.
Look out for the smile of thousands,
Each and every heart-breaking, shouting.
In a long-endless way it goes,
This is what I know.
Carry options on my way,
Their joy makes my day.
Forgiving every small mistakes,
And every promise that breaks.
All those crashing headaches,
Can never be replaced.
Two option, which one do I take?
I choose kindness,
Cause it is my way.

79. THE MAGIC OF WINTER

ANOOJA NAIR
GRADE 11A SCIENCE

The melting ice on top of flakes,
The coldest dust upon the gaze.
Path of the mountain climber covered in ice,
The whole journey dawn upon dusk.
Million of walk backs,
And plenty of tasks.
Cold as thick ice,
It has different faces like dice.
The way it brings the cold and shivers,
Joy in hours with blankets – the surrender!

80. NOT A HUMAN YET STILL THE SAME

ANOOJA NAIR
GRADE 11A SCIENCE

I'm not that different,
Name I call myself.
When people give up on me,
I still bow and touch.
I was born with pride and worship flows through my blood,
Money is not something I value than help.
Giving is what I learn every day,
Something you can't provide but always say.
I'm not that different,
I breath, eat, talk and sleep like every human.
I was given equality the day I was born,
By god, my savior, I'm drowned in my faults.
I was forgiven for my every mistake I made,
That's my right to be a human and not the same.

81. Growing older
ANOOJA NAIR
GRADE 11A SCIENCE

It was a sin,
It had gone on the spin.
Since they were just ten,
The story continued as they started it again.
They met while playing at the park,
It was without leaving a mark.
Near the swing, in the sand pit,
They both build up a tiny sand castle.
He gave her a small remark,
While her baby eyes had sparks.

All the other kids looked at her and laughed,
When he pushed her face down to the sand.
Her fun-size eyes were filled with water
and she did not know what to do,
She felt ashamed for trusting him.
Standing up from the pit she ran to her mother,
Curling up against the young lad's knee.
He felt guilty for doing it but rather than a word said,
He let it slid and continued his own business.
His little pals patting his back in support for what he did,
But he pushed them and left to find his missing fit.

82. If the pet was a person
ANOOJA NAIR
GRADE 11A SCIENCE

Nickel and dime,
Well upholstered,
She wished that he was a man.
The buddy lifted his tail up and down in happiness,
This tiny friend was enough to solve a millions of problems.

He was brown and had soft rabbit-like fur,
A small blank small left for his nose.
His body was covered in fur,
Always ended up looking like a bear.
His paws were very tiny as he was only a year old,
He too had lost his mother as she got old.

In the cold, rainy days,
He cuddled with her.
In the summer days,
He waited by the door, wanting her to come back quick.
When the yellow leaves fell down,
He was curled up near her feet,
Making her his first priority.
It was the love of an owner and a dog.

83. The place visited often
ANOOJA NAIR
GRADE 11A SCIENCE

The white building stood in the middle of nowhere,
Leaves covered this old, dusty and rusty place.
Walking into the room gracefully,
She sat down by the bench.
The little blue dress falling down to the ground,
Touching her cold smooth feet.

The art of the place was calm and quiet,
Just accordingly to the climate.
She closed her pretty eyelids,
And shut down her trembling lips.
Holding her hands interlined,
She prayed and prayed till sunset.
All mighty gods and their enchanting prayers,
Preaching into her head unbearable to hear.
She felt the quiet ambience and all the sources,
It was attracting her even more.
It had some sort of magic,
She instantly wanted to recover from her tragic.
This was her home to where besides,
The place she visited often reside.

84. Love song
ANOOJA NAIR
GRADE 11A SCIENCE

Love song that is overheard,
He is jealous.
He doesn't want to talk,
She is messing up with him.
For a very long time,
He thought to give up.
Wanting for her is keeping him alive.
He is done, doomed and not wanting to come back,
He is hurt but silent,
He doesn't want to speak back.
He is funny, emotional and caring,
But all he needs is a little bit of love.
This is not just at the moment,
But thousands of emotions that has gotten together,
And are way afar from catching the dreams.
He plugged in his earphones,
Just as his heart was plugged.
An another day of mystery,
About to be solved.
Life with fights,
Reminds him of the life with harmony.

85. The day someone surprised
ANOOJA NAIR
GRADE 11A SCIENCE

It was not all about streamers and pop-ups,
It was not all about candles and small lamps.
Holdings of memories were a guise,
The book of laws of emotion was now almost disguised.
An old lady, in a baggy trench coat,
With a red poplin hat and rain boots
stood in front of the door.
Even though it wasn't pouring,
she held an umbrella to serve her head from the heat.
She stood next to the door with a long warm smile,
The young women seemed worried but let the lad in.
"I have come from a land far, far away to see you"
"I am Mrs. Westwood!"
The young lady welcomed her in
and went to get her a cup of tea,
By the time she comes back, the lad finds her in a room
full of gifts and letters,
Feeling thankful she turns around to check
what had happen but did not find the lady.
Sadly, she turned back to find the tea gone,
Surprised she turned back again to find
the old lady in front of her.
Looking into her hands, she realized
Mrs. Westwood had something in her hands.
Looking up to her eyes,
She saw the twinkles, the best birthday surprise.

86. Restored faith

ANOOJA NAIR
GRADE 11A SCIENCE

Now, it was time to take back the fear,
As it has been restored.
Faith was just a belief,
It was brighten by the race and light.
He finally felt happiness in and about,
He finally felt redeemed but didn't last long.

This time was different than any other story,
The track had changed its way.
He thought of giving up multiple times
but didn't find a way to get out,
Feeling tired, he went for a nap.
He saw a dream of fortune,

In a wonderland he went.
He saw the stars and saw the clouds,
He saw all the trouble around the world.
He saw the moon, and saw the sun,
He saw all the creatures of the world.
Felling mistaken he went to sleep
again and again he saw them.

87. The feeling of betrayal
ANOOJA NAIR
GRADE 11A SCIENCE

He woke up with a heart race,
Sweating from his foreheads and down.
Feeling immense betrayals,
From everyone including her.
Felt that she was near him but far away,
Their promises were all broken from then and afar.

Looked around the room,
Finding numerous pictures on the walls and everywhere.
His mind was full of her,
But he could not forget the greetings upon dawn.
On what she did to him as revenge,
Where it was all broken off.

Life without trouble is a misery,
Life without pain is a disease.
She had broken them all,
While they fell apart piece by piece.
She had cheated on him not once, not twice,
But for years and regrets were all he thoughts.
His side without mistakes were a blemishing pain.

88. HUERFANO

ANOOJA NAIR
GRADE 11A SCIENCE

What is it to be orphaned?
Have you thought to yourself?
 What pain does it feel?
To be one?
You must have a dream.
They feel very lonely,
They have no one to love,
But they have God.
That is more than enough.

They become more than stronger
 They become more successful
They have more dreams
They are to be cared.
Even when they go through,
They are well disciplined
They feel very lonely
They don't know their values
They are the gems in the world
 God's hands they are gold.

89. CATHERINE
ANOOJA NAIR
GRADE 11A SCIENCE

Oh Catharine, Oh my dear.
Don't be upset,
From moon till you learn.
When you reach the time of life,
Oh Catharine, Oh my dear.
It's the entire wall against time.
Where hatred is not beyond,
Tell them what you know today.
Tell them you won't have prejudice.
When you know the truth,
Don't be restless.
Keep it on.

Oh Catharine, Oh my dear.
Don't regret.
From the dark till the sun.
 Way to find,
To find your way.
Oh Catharine, Oh my dear.
When your time comes don't push away.
Know what you did,
Spell what you say.
Every day life teaches you a new lesson,
So will I.
Remember that I' am here
And forget the past.
Wonder when you know,
Wonder what you did.

Oh Catharine, Oh my dear.
Don't neglect.

From heaven till your day.
Happiness cannot be changed,
But you should know who you are.
Oh Catharine, Oh my dear.
Once, you reach down to land,
 Once, upon you live.
With no other words I said.
Be free from Brobdingnagian robustness.
When dawn comes upon the night.
The light falls upon your head.
And God shall help you.

Oh Catherine, Oh my dear.
 Don't leave your dreams.
I may not be there,
But heaven is ready for you.
Do not dwell over the past,
Use your shrewdness Delphic.
 More on your future,
Helps you take care.
Leave the rest to who you believe,
It must not be Maw.
Your words must be useful,
Just as you are precious.
Find a reason to live,
A reason for your existence.
Then shall you succeed,
When shall you proceed?
Listen to your soul,
That's what you need.
Search for what you lost,
By the track of time.
Oh Catharine, Oh my dear.
Never give up on what you hear.

90. Voctor

Bhadra Sudheer
11-C

As I stand in the ring,
My oponent comes in with a smug smile,
I look at him with a thought
"Oh this is easy"
My opponent hits first
And I stumble back,
"Oh no, this is not good"
I hit back more fierce than him
And he stumbles back very badly
I turn and look at my fans,
Cheering and applauding for me
And I look on and wave at them with a smile.
But then an unexpected blow comes from the back
As I stumbled back way worse than he had
"Oh no, I'm getting defeated"
But then I look at my fans cheering nonstop,
And draw encouragement from them,
And gave a mighty blow to my opponent,
And I watch as he falls down to this defeat.
And there I am,
Standing as a Victor!

91.   A glass of wine
ANOOJA NAIR
GRADE 11A SCIENCE

I took a sip of the good old wine,
From, my mood aroused divine.
Who am I?
I want to define,
To those who mock me from behind.
I keep my head up to say I'm fine,
I'm not, even with all-stars combined.
I can't remove all of my pain,
Therefore I am stuck within the strong cage.
No more years to sit and whine,
Happiness is nowhere to find.
Like a dead body,
I lay on the floor,
Head suffering from a hurricane.
I feel like my life is on the deadline,
Nothing shall the human do that's kind.

92. Drunk and sorrowful
ANOOJA NAIR
GRADE 11A SCIENCE

The glass piece pierced through my skin,
Her shadow left me another sin.
The rose petals on the floor gave me shrills,
My mind could never take that much in.
Like a rose flower,
The thorns were poking me, provoking me to die.
I had to hold on,
Because for me, there is no one to cry upon.
I can only whine all day,
But my fate is never going to change.
One day more,
Is like one day less to explore.
I was dead from the inside,
My body felt tied.
Hot tears down my cheeks,
Had me crying for weeks.
The pain was too much to hold,
A story untold.
Life not worth as gold was my last breath on being bold.
What have I gotten myself into?
What sin have I committed?
The number of days to live is less,
God, love me some more.

93. Mother Earth

Bhadra Sudheer
11-C

Mother Earth falling down the steps of
destruction,
Due to us humans.
We shall take part
In saving our mother
By doing some steps on our own.
We shall make our mother greener,
cleaner and bluer,
By saving water,
By planting trees,
By not dumping waste,
So that, we living beings,
And our future, may stay safe..
We shall spend our blood, sweat and
tears,
In saving our Mother Earth

94. The earnings of life
ANOOJA NAIR
GRADE 11A SCIENCE

I get respect when I work well,
Trapped inside a door less shell.
My earnings are always important,
As I feel my life has shortened.
As my income goes higher and higher.
I start to dream and desire.
My heart burning like a fire,
Weird sounds through my head like choir.
My soul throbbing with throes,
Knowing that my end is close.
I feeling that I ought to a propose,
My feelings have froze.
My head aching from the bawling,
I had to save myself and my belongings.
Going on and on exploring,
My life is on the line that someone is calling.
An eye speaking a million lies,
It is me who I am going to prioritize.
Everyday feels like a Monday,
Where originality has stunned me.
Everybody judges me based on my money,
But nobody knows I am lonely.